THAT BABY IS NO FUN

Written By
Nettie Thomas-Lark

Illustrated By Brenda Pinkston

This book is dedicated to:
My grandsons, Melisizwe (Mellie) Charles Lark and
Jomo Lee Lark who inspired me to write this book.
and
In Memory Of
Melisizwe and Jomo's maternal South African Xhosa
(Koh-suh) grandmother, Nomgcobo (Nomi) Sangweni.

Special Thanks:
Editors:
Jean Smith Andrews, published children book author
Dr. Jean Harvey, Sociologist
Dr. Virginia Noville, Institute For Effective Educators
Nettie Williams, Adjunct Professor, NY Institute Of Technology
Children Editors: Kyndall Bailey, Nicholas Bailey, and Aris Pinkston
Art Editor:
Crystal Pinkston

© Copyright: by Nettie Thomas-Lark
2021 Second Edition
Illustrations in colored pencil and markers by Brenda Pinkston
Book Cover Design by Brenda Pinkston

Published by Sweet Sassafras Publication LLC
Charlotte, North Carolina
www.sweetsassafraspublication.com

No part of this book can be copied or reproduced without
the express consent of the author under penalty of US Copyright Law.
Library of Congress Control Number 2011919691

ABOUT THE BOOK

"That Baby Is No Fun" is a colorful and educational reading experience for young children crafted through the perspective of the author's grandson, Mellie. Her humorous story-telling style helps children identify with one of the single most impacting events in their lives, the arrival of a new sibling. The book can be read-aloud by parents, teachers, caregivers, and childcare provides or by children ages 3 to 8. By using age-appropriate words and pictures, the author and illustrator keep children engaged and broaden their understanding of family growth.

Children will be able to relate to the range of emotions Mellie feels as he await the arrival of his baby brother. From its inception, the story builds through the eyes and thoughts of a precocious three-year old boy. At times, he is sad, hopeful, confused, joyful and even afraid when he ponders what having a baby brother really means. Children will connect with the love expressed by Mellie's father, mother and grandmother as they bond with him to ease his fears and expectations about the baby's birth.

Although Mellie and his family live in an urban American city, "That baby Is No Fun" exposes readers to some small aspects of the family's African culture. Children from all backgrounds will be intrigued by the sound and meanings of the African terms, which are explained in the glossary. This gentle yet insightful story will make children want to read this book again and again.

Dr. Jean P. Harvey, Sociologist

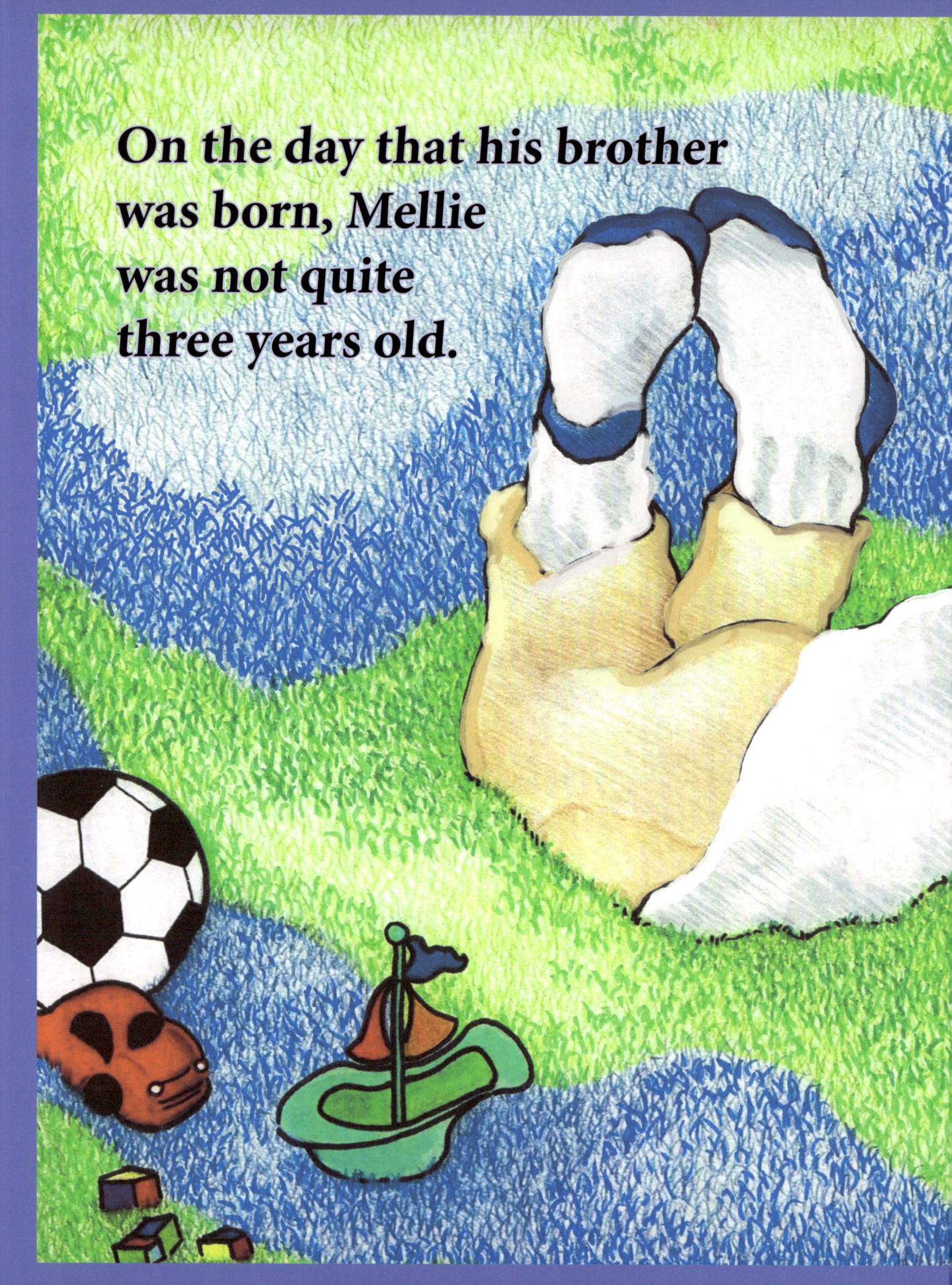

On the day that his brother was born, Mellie was not quite three years old.

Dad was helping Mellie get dressed for preschool. Mellie did not want to go to school that day. He was excited about getting a little brother soon.

He said, "Daddy, I'm not going to school anymore until my brother is born! I'm going to stay home with Mama!"

Dad smiled and gave him a hug. He told Mellie not to worry about Mama and the baby. I will be here with them all day. You must go to school.

It was a cold and windy day in the city. Dad told Mellie to go get his coat, gloves, hat, scarf and boots. Slowly, Mellie walked over to where Mama kept his things. He sat on the floor trying to put on his boots.

Dad said, "Mellie don't be upset. Let me help you finish getting dressed." Mellie said, "I can put them on all by myself!"

Dad gave Mellie his lunchbox.
He buckled him in his car seat and off to preschool they went.

All day long Mellie talked and daydreamed about seeing his brother soon. He imagined how he would play with him the moment he got home from the hospital.

Mellie remembered how each night Mama would read a story to him and his unborn brother. Some nights she would play the guitar and sing a song in her native African Zulu and Xhosa (Koh-suh) languages.

Mellie wondered if the baby could hear her voice in there. One night he asked Mama if he could hear her. She said, "Yes, Mellie, he can hear me." That made him very happy.

When Dad picked Mellie up from preschool that afternoon, he told him that he had a surprise. Mellie said, "I know! I know! I'm going to see my brother today!"

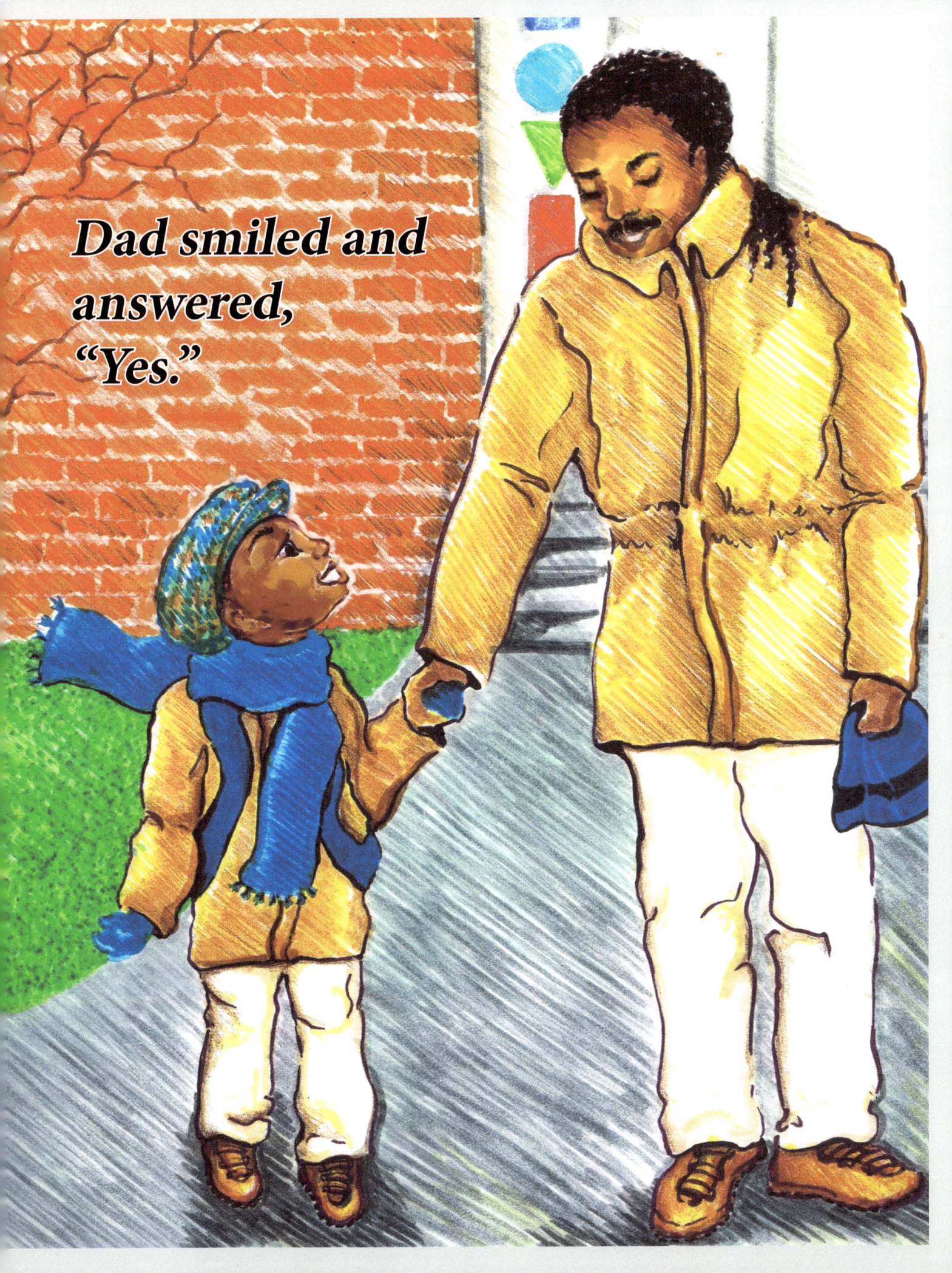

Mellie talked and cheered all the way to the hospital. He talked to Dad about how he was going to let his brother play with his toys when he comes home. Dad listened to him and said, "Mellie, the baby is too young to play with toys right now." Mellie was too excited to hear what Dad said.

When they arrived at the hospital, Dad and Mellie rode in the elevator upstairs. Mama and his little brother were waiting for them.

Mellie ran to get a look at his brother. Mama said, "this is Jomo. He is named for a very famous African Freedom Fighter."

He began to talk to him, kiss and squeeze his cheeks. Mama told Mellie to be careful not to squeeze too hard. Mellie wanted Jomo to wake up. All Jomo wanted to do was sleep. Mellie thought Jomo was not happy to see him.

It was time for Dad and Mellie to go home. He whispered to Jomo, "when you come home I'm going to let you play with my toys but you have to wake up Jomo!"

The next day Mama and Dad brought Jomo home from the hospital. Mellie was clapping and shouting, "Yipee!" He thought, now Jomo will wake up and play with me.

When Mellie realized that Jomo was not going to wake up and play with him, he was sad. That night his grandmother, (Gogo) called from South Africa. She is from the Xhosa (Koh-suh) people.

She asked to speak with Mellie. Gogo said, "Hello grandson. I know you are excited to see your brother!"

Mellie was quiet for a minute. Then he said, "Gogo, THAT BABY IS NO FUN! All he does is sleep! I think he is shy! He can't even play with me!"

After a while Mellie started to sing along with Gogo. When they finished singing the lullaby, Gogo and Mellie sang it to Jomo.

Mama, Dad and Mellie looked at Jomo. Jomo had a little smile on his face. Mellie said, "Yay! Jomo is happy that I am his brother! I love you Jomo!"

Mellie held it up for Jomo to see. He said, "when you get big like me, I am going to let you play with my toys and even ride my bike!"

Zulu Lullaby

Thula thula thula baba,
Thula thula thula san.
Thul' u babuz ficka, eku seni.
Kukh' in khan-yezi, zi-holel' u baba
Kim-khan yi-sela indlel'e ziyak-haya,
Thula thula thula baba,
Thula thula thula san.

~ English Translation~

Keep quiet my baby,
Keep quiet my child.
Be quiet, daddy will be home by dawn
There's a star that will lead him home
The star will brighten his way home,
Keep quiet my baby,
Keep quiet my child.

Glossary

Gogo: A term of endearment used to describe a grandmother in South African culture.

Jomo: The name given to the second child in the story. Jomo is named for the Kenyan freedom fighter, Jomo Kenyatta who fought to free Kenya from colonial rule. He became the first president of Kenya.

Melisiwze (Mellie) is a South African Zulu name, which means "leader of a nation."

Xhosa: (Koh-suh) A nation of people who live in Southern Africa with similar language and culture. Nelson Mandela and the grandmother (Gogo) were Xhosa.

Zulu: A nation of people with similar language and culture who live in Southern Africa. The mother of Melisiwze is from two diverse African cultures. She has a Zulu father and a Xhosa mother.

ABOUT THE AUTHOR

Nettie Thomas-Lark was born in Mobile, Alabama. She earned a Bachelor Degree in History from Alabama State University. She taught briefly in Mobile, before moving to New Jersey. Mrs. Lark soon realized she wanted to teach younger children so she decided to pursue her Elementary Education Certification from Jersey City State University. Later, she received a Master's degree from the same university. During her years in New Jersey, she worked exclusively in Elementary schools. Some years later, the author lived briefly in Maryland and South Carolina. While in South Carolina, she met and married Charles Lark Sr. and moved to Brooklyn, New York with him and his ten-year old son, Courtney. At the writing of this book, that ten-year-old boy is now an adult and married to Yolanda Sangweni, an amazing South African woman. He is the father in this true story, "That Baby Is No Fun." During her tenue in New York, Mrs. Lark continued to work as an Elementary teacher. Later, she became the Director of Staff Development for a School District and a Principal. While Director of Staff Development, she and a few dedicated teachers researched and publish curriculum material related to Black history as a supplement to the Social Studies and English Language Arts curriculum. In addition, during this time, the author attended Brooklyn College where she received a Professional Diploma in Supervision and Administration. For her exceptional work as Director of Staff Development, she received the Educator of the year Award for her school district in 2000 from the New York School City School Chancellor. One of the most important legacies of Mrs. Lark's tenue is that in 2002 she became the first principal of an inner city school in New York City to set-up a Robotics lab as well as, send a teacher to Robotics camp to be trained to teach students Robotics. She was and still is an innovator who thinks of creative ways to help young children improve their minds via creating children's books.

Together with her husband, Charles, they received numerous awards from various community organization for service to communities in Brooklyn. In 2005, the New York Daily News featured Mrs. Lark and her husband, Charles for outstanding service to others in Brooklyn. Presently, she is a member of Charlotte Alumnae Chapter of Delta Sigma Theta Sorority where she still gives service to her community. She has organized several book clubs, one of which members have given assistance to help others by donating gas cards to people looking for employment and monetary contributions to a local food bank to help feed the hungry.

The author retired as a principal from New York City. She lives in Charlotte, North Carolina. Presently, she is working on two other children books to complete a trilogy based on true experiences of the same character, Mellie. This trilogy of books will take young readers on a journey to new places and allow them to experience new things. They will enjoy and have fun as they read about Mellie's adventures again and again.

Sweetsassafraspublication.com

ABOUT THE ILLUSTRATOR

Brenda Pinkston is a native of New Jersey. She has a Bachelor of Arts Degree in Fine Arts and Advertising and Design from the College of New Jersey. Ms. Pinkston is a fine artist and a published children book illustrator. She worked several years as Art Director for Don Vereen's Applause. A woman's designer salon in New Jersey. It was at Applause that she mastered her art style by forcing pen and ink fashion illustrations to display a sense of gradual shading using vertical lines. This method has become her trademark. Her work has been featured in newspapers, magazines, billboards and various other print media. In addition, she was the art editor for a community-based newspaper and a web developer for the state of New Jersey's Office of Information Technology. While employed by the State, she stayed connected to the art community by painting and exhibiting her artwork.

Ms. Pinkston is a Contemporary Impressionist Artist. Her paintings have been selected for two prestigious juried art exhibitions in New Jersey; The Mercer County College gallery in 2005 and the College of New Jersey Gallery, Alumni Exhibition in 2010. She was selected to paint a response to John Bigger's The Market Place for the Mint Museum, Charlotte, NC. This work is pictured in the photo below. Additionally, she has exhibited her work in New York, New Jersey, Pennsylvania, Georgia, South Carolina and North Carolina. Most recently, she displayed pieces of her work at the Delta Authors on Tour event in Charlotte, and in a virtual Delta Jazz Brunch. Pieces of her art were recently featured in a short film. Presently, she is planning a one-woman show sometime this fall of 2021 at 9189 Gallery in Charlotte. Ms. Pinkston moved to Charlotte with her daughter, Aris. She enjoys living and working in her art studio gallery. She remains committed to painting fine art and creating wonderful children's book illustrations.

pinkstonsart.com

www.ingramcontent.com/pod-product-compliance
Lightning Source LLC
LaVergne TN
LVHW071029070426
835507LV00002B/85